ROUNDABOUT THEATRE COMPANY

Todd Haimes, Artistic Director
Harold Wolpert, Managing Director
Julia C. Levy, Executive Director

In association with

Tracy Aron   Al Parinello   Stefany Bergson

Present

Donna Murphy

in

THE PEOPLE IN THE PICTURE

BOOK AND LYRICS BY

Iris Rainer Dart

MUSIC BY

Mike Stoller AND Artie Butler

with

Alexander Gemignani   Christopher Innvar   Nicole Parker
Rachel Resheff   Hal Robinson   Lewis J. Stadlen   Joyce Van Patten   Chip Zien

Brad Bradley   Rachel Bress   Jeremy Davis   Emilee Dupre   Maya Goldman
Louis Hobson   Shannon Lewis   Andie Mechanic   Jessica Lea Patty   Megan Reinking
Jeffrey Schecter   Paul Anthony Stewart   Lori Wilner   Stuart Zagnit

SET DESIGN	COSTUME DESIGN	LIGHTING DESIGN	SOUND DESIGN	PROJECTION DESIGN
Riccardo Hernandez	Ann Hould-Ward	James F. Ingalls	Dan Moses Schreier	Elaine J. McCarthy

HAIR & WIG DESIGN	MAKEUP DESIGN	ORCHESTRATIONS	DANCE MUSIC ARRANGEMENTS	DIALECT COACH	FIGHT DIRECTOR
Paul Huntley	Angelina Avallone	Michael Starobin	Alex Lacamoire	Kate Wilson	Rick Sordelet

PRODUCTION STAGE MANAGER	PRODUCTION MANAGEMENT	CASTING	GENERAL MANAGER	EXECUTIVE PRODUCER
Peter Wolf	Aurora Productions	Jim Carnahan, C.S.A. & Stephen Kopel	Rebecca Habel	Sydney Beers

MUSICAL DIRECTION BY

Paul Gemignani

MUSICAL STAGING BY

Andy Blankenbuehler

DIRECTED BY

Leonard Foglia

Roundabout Theatre Company is a member of the League of Resident Theatres.
www.roundabouttheatre.org

ISBN 978-1-4584-1898-2

HAL•LEONARD® CORPORATION

7777 W. BLUEMOUND RD. P.O. BOX 13819 MILWAUKEE, WI 53213

Visit Hal Leonard Online at
www.halleonard.com

BREAD AND THEATRE

Lyrics by IRIS RAINER DART

Music by MIKE STOLLER

GANG:
We are the War-saw gang, we play the Shte-tl cir-cuit,
To towns so bat-tered and be-sieged the folks are skit-tish,
Chay-es-el Fish-er once made love to Stan-i-slavs-ky,

which is a lou-sy deal no mat-ter how you work it. Why do we
we bring the clas-sics and de-li-ver them in Yid-dish. It's hard to
al-so to Che-kov, Dos-to-ev-sky and Tchai-kov-sky. But beau-ty's

8

MATRYOSHKA

Lyrics by IRIS RAINER DART

Music by MIKE STOLLER

nev - er bro - ken 'cause they're made of oak.__ And un - like you and me,__ they're carved out

of a tree.__ But here's what they will miss:__ a chance to dance like this!

Allegro

THE DYBBUK

Lyrics by IRIS RAINER DART

Music by MIKE STOLLER

E♭m7 A♭7 D♭ B♭7 E♭m A♭7
Does-n't a Dyb-buk still have feel-ings, and if you prick us don't we
D♭ N.C. D♭7 N.C. G♭ E♭m7
DANCING RABBIS:
DYBBUK:
bleed? Zex, zi-ben, acht. No-bod-y ev-er likes a Dyb-buk,
A♭m7 D♭7 G♭ D♭m/F♭ E♭7 D♭/F E♭7/G
RABBIS:
DYBBUK:
I guess that comes as no sur-prise. Vo-de-o-do. The min-ute I show up, they
A♭m E♭7 C♭ A♭7 D♭7 D7♭5 D♭7
RABBIS:
DYBBUK:
RABBIS:
pan-ic. No, no, no. And then they rush to ex-or-cise. Hit the road!

REMEMBER WHO YOU ARE

Lyrics by IRIS RAINER DART

Music by ARTIE BUTLER

PINSKER:

Finger snaps

When Mu - ni
By mag - ic

Wei - sen-freund was turned in - to Paul Mu - ni, he had to play a guy who had an ug - ly

Er - ic Weiss be - came the great Hou - di - ni. As A - sa Yol - son, did Al Jol - son have a

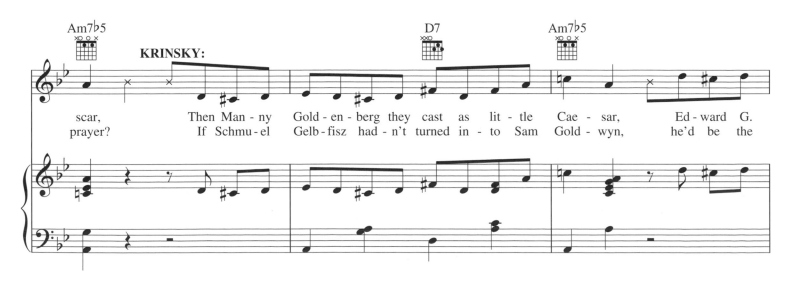

KRINSKY:

scar, Then Man - ny Gold - en - berg they cast as lit - tle Cae - sar, Ed - ward G.

prayer? If Schmu - el Gelb - fisz had - n't turned in - to Sam Gold - wyn, he'd be the

HOLLYWOOD GIRLS

Lyrics by IRIS RAINER DART

Music by MIKE STOLLER

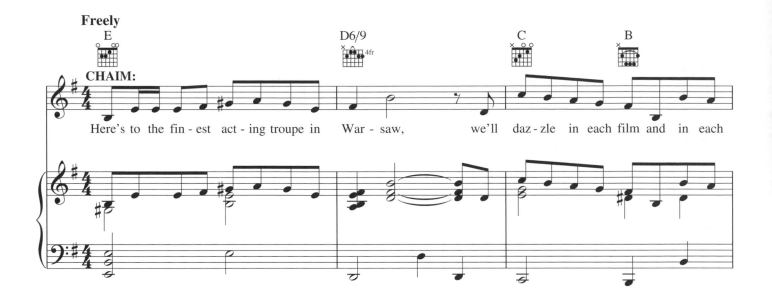

Here's to the fin-est act-ing troupe in War-saw, we'll daz-zle in each film and in each

play. Now in a twist of fate no-bod-y fore-saw, _____ they

want our tal-ents in the U. S. A. So

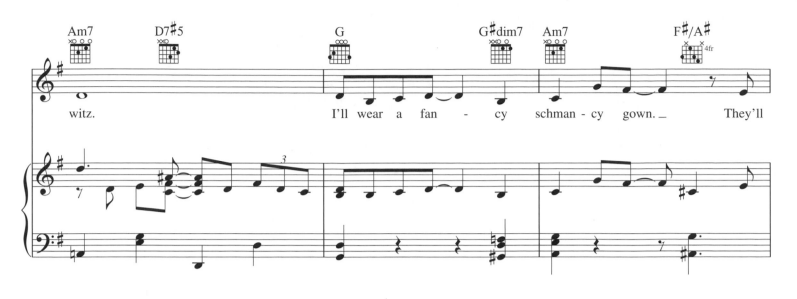

witz. I'll wear a fan - cy schman - cy gown. _ They'll

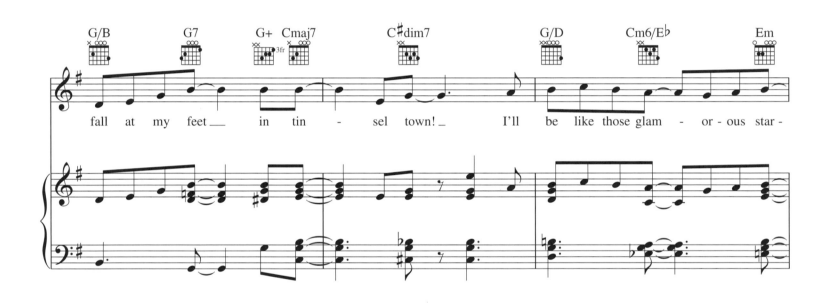

fall at my feet _ in tin - sel town! _ I'll be like those glam - or - ous star-

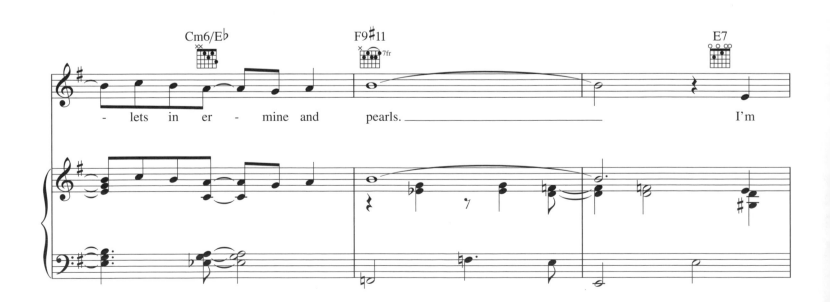

- lets in er - mine and pearls. _____ I'm

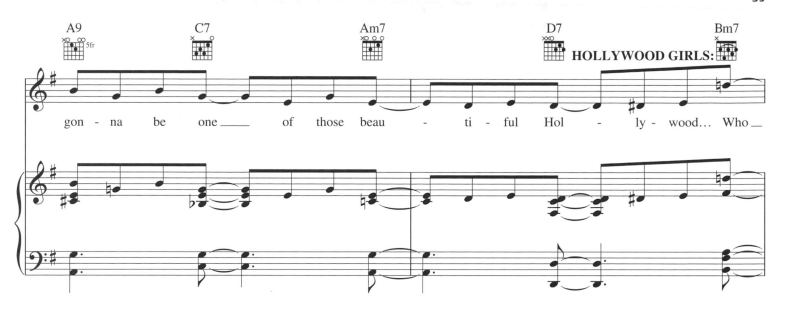

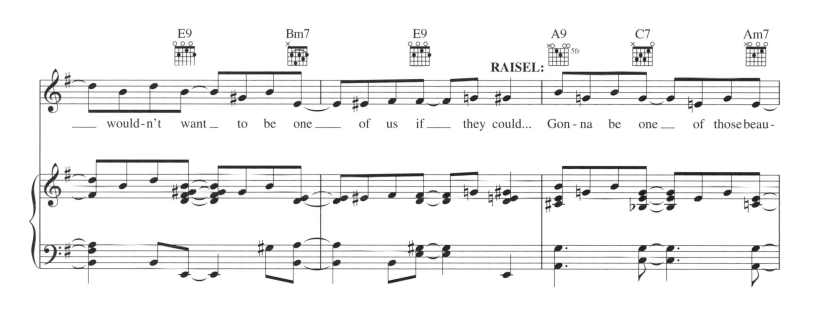

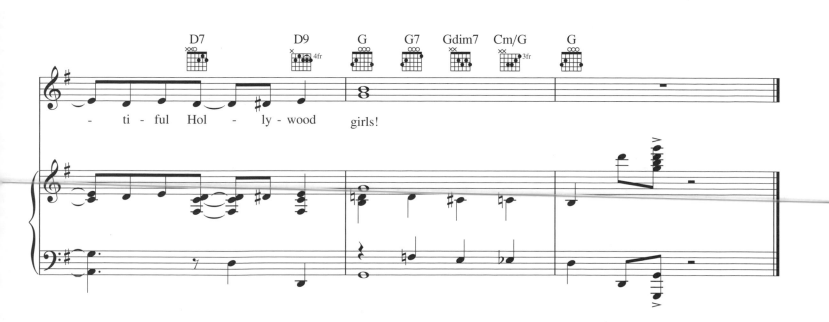

AND GOD LAUGHS

Lyrics by IRIS RAINER DART

Music by MIKE STOLLER

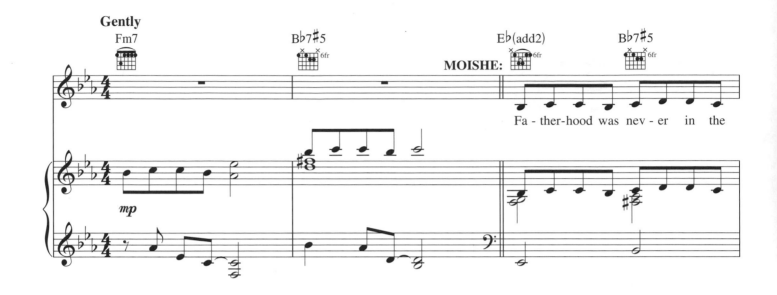

Fa - ther-hood was nev - er in the

cards for me. ___ Too bad, be - cause my heart's so full of love. ___ But

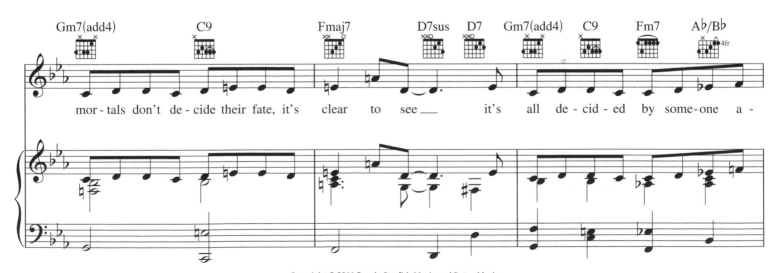

mor - tals don't de - cide their fate, it's clear to see ___ it's all de - cid - ed by some-one a -

RED'S DILEMMA
(Can I Really Leave You Here?)

Lyrics by IRIS RAINER DART

Music by MIKE STOLLER

FOR THIS

Lyrics by IRIS RAINER DART

Music by MIKE STOLLER

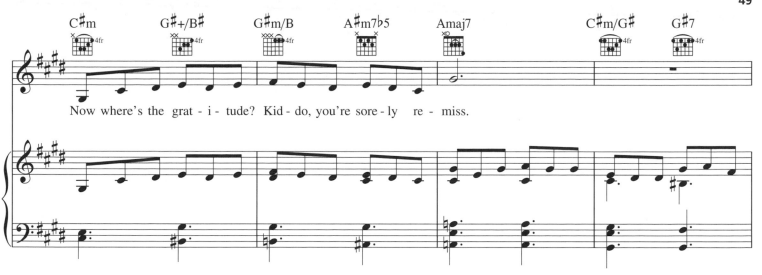

Now where's the grat - i - tude? Kid - do, you're sore - ly re - miss.

I kept on slav - ing to make your life sweet, _____ for

this?

RED:
Six kinds of ther - a - py o - ver the years, _____ for this?

WE WERE HERE

Lyrics by IRIS RAINER DART

Music by ARTIE BUTLER

58

NOW AND THEN

Lyrics by IRIS RAINER DART

Music by MIKE STOLLER

find the good in ev - 'ry - one. ___ And you can take a thing that's sad and spin it

round and make it fun. ___ If I was that way once, I can't re - mem - ber

when, 'cause this is now and that was then.

ICH, UCH, FEH

Lyrics by IRIS RAINER DART

Music by ARTIE BUTLER

RAISEL:

My friends, please let me tell you of my peo - ple. _____ Since
sounds you nev - er need some - one to tran - slate. _____ They

time be - gan, we al - ways ran to live in man - y lands. And
mean the same in ev - 'ry tongue from Par - is to Hong Kong. No

quick - ly we would learn the lo - cal lan - guage and then ex -
need to stud - y tens - es or de - clen - sions, no need to

SELECTIVE MEMORY

Lyrics by IRIS RAINER DART

Music by MIKE STOLLER

SAYING GOODBYE

Lyrics by IRIS RAINER DART

Music by ARTIE BUTLER

DOBRISCH:

learn, I watched you grow. To save your life, I let you go. You were a

ba - by, _____ I took you in and made _ you mine, you were my

treas-ure. _ I watched you chang-ing, I watched you learn, I watched you grow, _ know-ing the

day might come when I must let you go.

luck - y you're a - ble to live and be free and not at the bot - tom of

some ran - dom grave.

rit.

mf
a tempo

RED & CHILD: **add DOBRISCH:**

She brushed my hair, read me sto - ries and sang and we talked all

RED & CHILD: **add DOBRISCH:**

night.   She calmed my fears, kissed a - way all my tears,   and we'd

CHILD OF MY CHILD

Lyrics by IRIS RAINER DART

Music by MIKE STOLLER

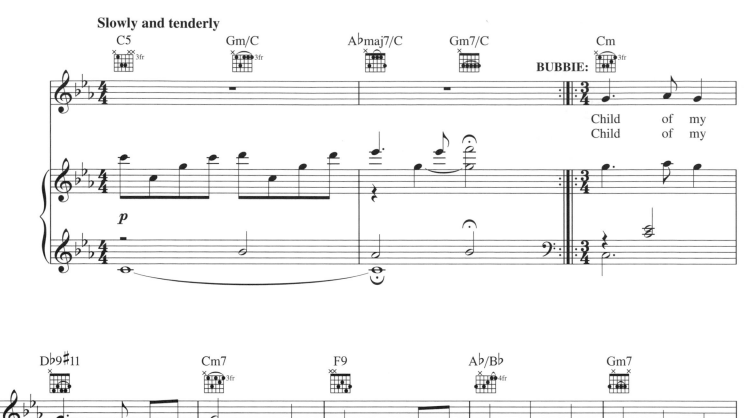

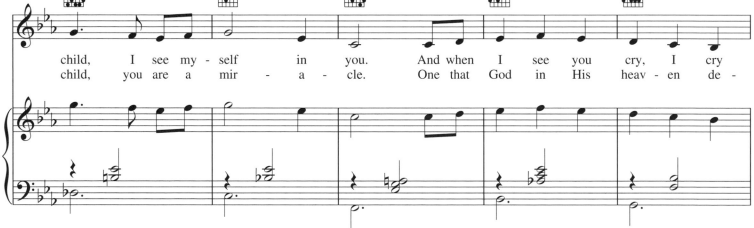